W9-ANA-624

BARD OF AVON
The Story of
William Shakespeare

DIANE STANLEY AND PETER VENNEMA

ILLUSTRATED BY DIANE STANLEY

MORROW JUNIOR BOOKS
New York

To Catherine,
my firstborn,
my thespian
D.S.

The authors would like to thank Dr. William B. Hunter,
who inspired this book and whose help was invaluable in writing it.

The full-color artwork was done in gouache, opaque watercolor paint,
on Fabriano watercolor paper. The text type is 14 point Bernhard Modern.

Text copyright © 1992 by Diane Stanley and Peter Vennema
Illustrations copyright © 1992 by Diane Stanley.

Printed in Singapore at Tien Wah Press.
11 12 13 14 15 16 17 18 19 20

Library of Congress Cataloging-in-Publication Data
Stanley, Diane.
Bard of Avon : the story of William Shakespeare / by Diane Stanley
and Peter Vennema ; illustrated by Diane Stanley.
p.   cm.
Includes bibliographical references.
Summary: A brief biography of the world's most famous playwright,
using only historically correct information.
ISBN 0-688-09108-3 (trade)—ISBN 0-688-09109-1 (library)—ISBN 0-688-16294-0 (pbk.)
1. Shakespeare, William, 1564–1616 Biography—Juvenile
literature 2. Dramatist, English–Early modern, 1500–1700—
Biography—Juvenile literature. [1.Shakespeare, William,
1564–1616. 2. Dramatists, English. 3. Poets, English.]
I. Vennema, Peter. II. Title.
PR2895.S7 1992
822.3'3—dc20 [92] [B]
90-46564 CIP AC

J B
SHAKESPEARE, W.

C. 2

Authors' Note

William Shakespeare is one of the most famous men who ever lived. Yet much of his life is a mystery to us. He did not keep a diary, and none of his personal letters has survived. We do not even know exactly when he was born—only the date on which his baptism was registered. We know a little about his parents, his wife, and his children. Besides his plays and poems, the only other documents we have are business transactions, court papers, and his will.

Of course, we know a great deal about the times in which he lived—of Queen Elizabeth and King James, and the great men who admired and encouraged Shakespeare's work. His friends and fellow writers have left us bits of information in their books and letters. After he died, many tales about his life were told, though we do not know which—if any of them—are true.

In writing this story, we have tried to show how historians investigate a life lived long ago. Like detectives, historians gather all the known facts together until a pattern begins to appear. And when that pattern reveals the life of one of the most exceptional writers of all time, what an exciting discovery that is!

IN THE YEAR 1569, A COMPANY OF TRAVELING ACTORS CAME TO THE LITTLE English town of Stratford-on-Avon. As their cart rolled into the town square, the high bailiff, or mayor, greeted the actors and led them to the guildhall where they would do a special performance for him. If he liked the play, he would give them a license to present it to the public.

The high bailiff was John Shakespeare, a prosperous glove maker. He was pleased and agreed to pay the Queen's Players nine shillings—less than fifty dollars today. Perhaps he allowed his five-year-old son, William, to sit in front with him for the special performance. If so, it was the first play he ever saw.

The actors were given permission to perform, so they began to unload their cart. They set out trestles in the courtyard of an inn and laid long boards over them for a stage. They hung a curtain behind it as a backdrop and took out their costumes and props. Soon they were ready to entertain the good folk of Stratford.

We don't know what play they performed. Perhaps they did *Ralph Roister Doister*, a funny play with characters named Matthew Merrygreek and Margery Mumblecrust. Or it may have been a tragedy about some great hero, with lots of sword fighting and dramatic speeches. Doubtless, the people loved it and talked about it long afterward, for public entertainment was rare in those days. From then on, traveling players came to Stratford almost every year, and it was always a special event.

When William was six or seven, he entered the local grammar school. It was a good school for its day, and it was free, though only boys could go. The schoolmaster taught the younger boys to read and write. In another part of the room, he led the older boys in the study of Latin and Greek. They memorized long passages of poetry in those languages. William had an amazing memory, and years later he frequently referred to the myths and history of his childhood study in the great plays he wrote.

William graduated from Stratford Grammar School when he was sixteen. By then, the Shakespeare family had fallen on hard times. John Shakespeare owed money. He could not pay his taxes. He was no longer a town leader and, at one point, didn't even go to church for fear of being arrested for debt. Obviously, there was no money for a university education.

So William Shakespeare went to work, but we don't know what he did. He probably helped his father make gloves, though some people think that he was a schoolmaster's assistant and others that he worked for a lawyer.

Only one thing is certain: when William Shakespeare was eighteen years old, he got married to Anne Hathaway, who was twenty-six. John and Mary Shakespeare were probably against the marriage. First of all, the family was short of money. And the house on Henley Street must have been crowded and noisy enough already, for William had three brothers and two sisters, and the youngest of them was only three. Even so, William brought his new wife to live with them, and when their daughter Susanna was born, six months later, there were ten people in the house. Less than two years later, there were twelve, when Anne gave birth to twins, Hamnet and Judith.

Some time after that, William left Stratford and went to London. No one knows when he left or under what circumstances.

Anne, Susanna, and the twins stayed behind in Stratford. We assume that Will sent money to support them, and came sometimes to visit. But he never took them to London to live with him, and he and Anne had no more children. It does not appear that they had a very happy marriage.

William Shakespeare went to London just at the time when modern theater was taking shape. In 1576, when Shakespeare was still a schoolboy, an actor named James Burbage put up a building near London designed solely for the performance of plays. It was the first such building since the days of ancient Greece and Rome. He called it the Theatre, a name now used for all playhouses.

The people of London loved to see plays, and James Burbage's Theatre was a smash success. Soon other playhouses were built, first the Curtain, then the Rose and the Swan.

These new theaters were circular wooden buildings with an open courtyard in the middle, much like the inn yards in which plays were often performed. People could stand in the courtyard for a penny. They were called groundlings, and they were known to drink too much beer and be quite noisy and rude if they didn't like the play. A wise playwright would throw in a joke every now and then to keep the groundlings happy.

Anyone willing to pay a bit more could sit in one of the three galleries, where they had a roof to protect them from the sun or a sudden shower.

Plays were only done in daylight and in nice weather, as there were no lights or heat. On the days when a play would be presented, a flag was flown from the tower of the theater, where people in the city could see it.

There was no curtain across the stage and not much scenery. A table and chairs would show that it was a banquet room; a potted bush would represent the countryside. Sometimes a sign was carried onstage telling the location, such as A WOOD NEAR ATHENS. Or an actor would walk onstage and say something such as, "Well, this is the Forest of Arden!"

The costumes were often elegant. In those days, it was customary for a gentleman to leave his clothes to his faithful servants when he died. But servants didn't wear that sort of clothing, so they sold it to the actors to wear as costumes.

A WOOD NEAR ATHENS

A Midsummer Night's Dream

The theaters also had special effects. The roof of the stage, painted with stars and called the heavens, had a trapdoor in it. If the play called for a god to descend from the sky, a throne could be lowered through the trapdoor by ropes. The sound of thunder was made by rolling a cannonball around on the floor of the hut above the stage. There was also a cannon up there that fired blanks for the battle scenes.

Just as there was a "heavens," there was also a "hell." This was the area under the stage, and it had a trapdoor, too, through which actors could appear or disappear as the play might require.

In Elizabethan plays, the death scenes were very realistic. The actor to be "stabbed" would hide a pouch of pig's blood under his shirt. This would burst when his opponent stabbed him, much to the delight of the groundlings.

Heavens

Hell

It is fortunate that Queen Elizabeth and her friends at court loved plays, for there was a powerful religious group, known as the Puritans, who wanted to close the theaters. The Puritans were very strict in their morals, and they thought plays were "sinful, heathenish, lewd, and ungodly." They also believed the theater attracted unruly crowds and criminals, which, in fact, it did.

The Puritans might have put an end to this new art if the queen and her courtiers had not given the actors their protection. A nobleman would adopt a company of actors and allow them to make use of his name, such as the Admiral's Men or Lord Chamberlain's Men. At one time, even Elizabeth had her own actors, the Queen's Men. In return, the actors would give special performances for their patron, either in the great halls of their estates or at the palace. The prestige of their patron's name went with them, even when acting in one of the new theaters or touring in the countryside.

In spite of all the influential help, the Puritans still managed to drive the players outside the London city limits, where all the famous Elizabethan theaters were built.

Each acting company had about twelve men, who often stayed together for years. There would always be a leading man and a comedian, as well as someone (like Shakespeare) who played "kingly" and older men's parts. There were also character actors and boy apprentices.

Shakespeare had to keep in mind the actors who would perform his play: whether they were young or old, thin or fat, and what sort of parts they played best.

All the players were men, as it was not considered proper for women to be actors. Women's parts were played by boys who were young enough to have a high voice and, of course, no beard.

The company would hire extra actors for small parts and crowd scenes. Since the plays often called for music, musicians were also hired.

The new theaters couldn't keep on doing the same stale farces and melodramas that had charmed country audiences. They needed fresh material, something more sophisticated for city people who went to the theater regularly.

Soon a group of brilliant and educated young men began putting their talents to writing plays. These University Wits, as they were called, wrote complicated and beautiful stories with magnificent poetry and lots of action. The greatest of these young playwrights was Christopher Marlowe.

When we pick up Shakespeare's trail again, in 1592, we find that he is working in London as an actor and has written a play, *Henry VI*. It must have been a popular play, for one of the Wits was so jealous, he described Shakespeare in a pamphlet as "an upstart crow, beautified with our feathers." He was insulted that a common actor would presume to write plays.

Despite the wits, Shakespeare had gotten his start as an actor and a playwright. But soon, an outbreak of the plague hit London, and all the theaters were closed for two years. The authorities believed that large gatherings of people would spread the disease.

Shakespeare took this time to write two long poems, *Venus and Adonis* and *The Rape of Lucrece*. He dedicated them to the Earl of Southampton, who paid him handsomely for the honor. Shakespeare was very grateful to Southampton for paying him so well. From that time on, he would never be poor again. And he would remain loyal to the young earl in the difficult times ahead.

It may have been during these early years that Shakespeare wrote his series of short poems, or sonnets—though they were published much later. Some of the poems were written to a "fair youth" and others to a "dark lady." There was also a "rival poet." Historians have been trying ever since to discover who these important people in Shakespeare's life might have been.

When, in 1594, the theaters reopened, Shakespeare had written at least five plays and would write several more that year.

He invested the generous gift from the Earl of Southampton in James Burbage's acting company, the Lord Chamberlain's Men. From then on, he was a partner and entitled to keep a percentage of the profits. His plays helped make the company popular and made Shakespeare a famous and wealthy man.

What kind of writer was Shakespeare? Most of his plots were not original. He found them in storybooks and in the pages of history. He breathed life into the main characters, added new ones, and changed the plot as his imagination prompted him. He wrote quickly—which must have helped the flow of his ideas—and he rarely revised his work. Though he sometimes made mistakes in haste, he didn't worry overly much about them. He knew his actors would make changes once they began to rehearse. He was writing for them, not for the printed page.

Shakespeare wrote three different kinds of plays: tragedies, comedies, and histories. In writing them, he followed many of the customs and fashions of the time.

The main characters in the tragedies, for example, were always doomed to death in the end. The comedies were full of mistaken identities, women disguised as men, miscarried letters, and all sorts of silly complications that were all resolved in the end, with everyone planning weddings. The histories told the stories of kings and great noblemen in exciting situations, such as war or rebellion.

Yet, while he followed all these conventions, he wove humor into his tragedies, put serious problems into his comedies, and brought the issues of the common people into his histories. His characters and the words they spoke were amazing and highly original.

Each of these wonderful plays had a central role for the company's leading man—James Burbage's son, Richard. In the early days, he played such youthful roles as Romeo in *Romeo and Juliet* and Prince Hal in *Henry IV*. As he grew older, he played Hamlet, Othello, King Lear, and Macbeth. It is unlikely that any other actor in history has been given such a series of great parts to play!

Richard III

The Tempest

Romeo and Juliet

Shakespeare's histories were very popular with the English people, partly because they were about English kings. Most historical plays at that time were about ancient civilizations, such as those of Greece or Rome. While Shakespeare wrote two such plays—*Julius Caesar* and *Antony and Cleopatra*—most of his histories were about the great (and not so great) kings of England as well as other heroes and villains, plots, murders, and battles out of England's history.

In doing research for *Henry IV*, he read that the king's son, Prince Hal, had been very wild in his youth. And so, with this little hint from history, Shakespeare's wonderful imagination invented Sir John Falstaff, a fat and drunken knight who leads Prince Hal astray. Though Falstaff is a shameless liar, loud, cowardly, and crude, somehow Shakespeare makes us love him. Falstaff is the butt of many jokes, but they never get him down. Even in the tense battle scenes, he is there, a ridiculous figure clanking around in enormous armor, trying to avoid danger at all cost.

The groundlings loved him, and so did everyone else. In fact, Queen Elizabeth asked Shakespeare to write another play about Falstaff, showing him in love. And so he wrote *The Merry Wives of Windsor*, in which Falstaff writes love letters to two different ladies. By chance, the ladies discover what he is up to and decide to get even. The poor fellow winds up hidden in a basket of dirty laundry, which is dumped in the Thames River.

Henry IV

The role of Falstaff was probably first played by Will Kempe, the popular comedian. Many of Shakespeare's plays had a "fool" role for Kempe, usually some kind of country bumpkin. Judging by the parts Shakespeare wrote for him, his acting must have been very broad, verging on slapstick.

In *Hamlet*, a group of traveling actors are cautioned to make sure their comedian does not interrupt the play by making faces or shouting silly remarks, just to get a laugh from the crowd. Some people think Shakespeare had Will Kempe in mind when he wrote those lines.

Kempe left the company after some kind of a disagreement. He then performed what today we would call a publicity stunt. He announced that he would dance all the way from London to Norwich—111 miles. When he had done it, he wrote a book about his adventure, called *Kempe's Nine Days' Wonder*.

To replace him, the company hired a new comedian named Robert Armin. He was a far more subtle actor than Will Kempe had been, and the comic parts Shakespeare wrote began to change. Now his "fools" became complex characters instead of buffoons. There was some sadness and tenderness mixed in with the comedy. For Robert Armin, Shakespeare wrote three of his greatest "fool" roles: Touchstone in *As You Like It*, Feste in *Twelfth Night*, and the Fool in *King Lear*. Though these "fools" spoke nonsense and made jokes, they also spoke great wisdom and touched our hearts.

Robert Armin must also have been musical, for Shakespeare gave him many lovely songs to sing.

Will Kempe

Robert Armin

The year 1599 brought a great event into Shakespeare's life—the building of the new theater that would be forever linked to his name.

The lease had run out on the land where James Burbage's Theatre stood. The building was twenty-three years old, and too small besides. When the landlord demanded more rent for his land, Richard Burbage and his brother, Cuthbert, decided to build another playhouse. They leased land across the Thames River from London, near the Rose and the Swan. Then they arranged for a carpenter named Peter Street to go into the Theatre by night and loosen the joints that held the building together.

On the night of January 20, the actors and their friends, some of them armed, "did . . . in most forcible and riotous manner take and carry away from there all the wood and timbers." That is how the landlord put it when he sued them. But the Burbages won the court case, since the landlord owned only the land, not the building.

They carried the boards across the frozen river to the new site. There they built the finest theater London had ever seen. Its sign showed a picture of Hercules holding the world on his shoulders, and it was called the Globe.

People flocked to the Globe to see Shakespeare's plays. Soon after one o'clock on fine days, London Bridge would be crowded with playgoers. Others were taxied across the river by the boatmen who were always ready and waiting at playtime.

In that first year, they did three new plays at the Globe: *As You Like It*, a comedy; *Henry V*, a history; and *Julius Caesar*, a tragedy. There were plenty of old plays to put on, too.

The Globe

In 1601, politics and danger entered Shakespeare's world. The events of that year seem to have touched him very deeply.

This is what happened: The Earl of Essex was one of Queen Elizabeth's great favorites. He was a dashing young nobleman who was fond of adventure and battle and was said to be the most popular man in England. But his life had taken strange turns, and that year he decided to mount a rebellion and overthrow the queen.

Essex's best friend was the Earl of Southampton, Shakespeare's old patron. He, too, was in on the plot.

Two days before the uprising was to take place, several of Essex's friends went to the Globe and offered forty shillings for a special performance of *Richard II* on the following day.

Richard II is one of Shakespeare's early plays. In it, an unfit king, Richard, is forced to give up his throne to a noble character, Bolingbroke, who then becomes Henry IV. Essex hoped that the crowds watching the play would think of him as a sort of Bolingbroke and be inspired to join him on the following day. To add to the effect, Essex's friends clapped and cheered at all the right moments, hoping to stir the crowd.

The next day, when Essex rode through the streets of London to raise the revolution, the people just closed their doors. Essex and his friends were arrested, and most of them were put to death. Southampton was allowed to live, but he was imprisoned in the Tower of London.

Queen Elizabeth knew about the special performance of *Richard II*, and understood the reason for it. "I am Richard II, know ye not that!" she was heard to say. The actors were questioned under oath but not punished. Forty shillings seemed to be a strong enough reason for a troupe to put on an old play by special request. The queen was willing to believe that they hadn't done it for political reasons.

Richard II

During these years, a profound change seems to have come over Shakespeare, and we see it in the plays he wrote. Perhaps he was frightened by his close brush with danger. He must have been horrified to think that the dashing Essex was dead, and his friend shut up in the Tower. It was also during this period that Shakespeare's father died. Now, instead of happy, romantic comedies, he began to create his great tragedies: *Hamlet, Othello, King Lear, Macbeth,* and *Antony and Cleopatra.* In each of these stories, a great man is brought to destruction and death. His fall is caused partly by forces of evil and partly by some flaw in the hero. And both *Hamlet* and *Macbeth* are about plots to murder kings.

Even his few comedies written in these years became darker, as if he had come to think badly of mankind.

In 1603, Queen Elizabeth died. The new king, James I, was a man who loved entertainment, and especially plays. His first week in London, he took over the patronage of Shakespeare's company. From then on, they were called the King's Men.

James I was also the king of Scotland. And for this Scottish king, Shakespeare turned to Scottish history to write *Macbeth,* one of his greatest plays. In it, he included many touches to please the king. There are witches and ghosts, bloody murders and mad scenes. But even with all the special effects, it is a dark and profound study of human nature.

Macbeth is a brave and loyal soldier until the witches tell him that he will someday be king. Ambition begins to burn in his heart, and he goes on to murder the king and everyone else who stands in the way of his goal. *Macbeth* is a chilling tale of a good man gone wrong, whose every step leads him closer and closer to his own destruction. It fascinated the playgoers of Shakespeare's time, and it fascinates us today.

Macbeth

When Shakespeare was about forty-seven, he left his busy life in London and retired to Stratford. There he lived the life of a country gentleman, in a grand house called New Place. This was a tranquil time.

Though his son Hamnet had died, his daughter Susanna had married and given him a granddaughter, Elizabeth. In a few years, the youngest daughter, Judith, also married. William and Anne seem to have lived together quietly, if not lovingly, after so many years apart.

From Stratford, he wrote his last few plays. There is a gentle quality about them, and a love of the countryside, which suggests that William Shakespeare had found peace in the village of his childhood.

On July 29, 1613, the first performance of his play *Henry VIII* took place at the Globe theater. In it, there is a scene where the king makes a grand entrance that is announced by firing a cannon. A spark accidentally set fire to the thatched roof, and within an hour, the famous Globe theater had burned to the ground. No one was hurt, but one man's pants caught on fire and had to be put out with the aid of a bottle of beer.

The King's Men hurriedly rescued props, costumes, and papers from the burning building. Fortunately for us, Shakespeare's plays were among the things they saved.

The theater was soon rebuilt, but William Shakespeare would not write any more plays for it. He lived the rest of his life quietly in the country.

Shakespeare's friends and admirers came to Stratford to see him. It was after a "merry meeting" with friends, including the playwright Ben Jonson, that he took sick with a fever.

In March 1614, he made his will. He left money to the poor of Stratford and to his friends. To his sister and his daughters, he gave his land, houses, and belongings. To his wife, Anne, he willed only his second-best bed! Historians have never quite known what to make of that.

He died on April 23, 1616. Though we do not know the exact date of his birth, it is quite possible that he died on his fifty-second birthday.

On the wall above his tomb is a sculpture of him, looking plump and middle-aged, writing with a quill pen. On the tomb are these lines:

> Good frend for Jesus sake forbeare,
> To digg the dust encloased heare:
> Blese be the man who spares thes stones,
> And curst be he who moves my bones.

Over the years, there have been people who could not believe that the son of a glove maker, a small-town boy with only a grammar-school education, could have written the greatest series of plays in the English language. These doubters have suggested that some of the famous men of the day wrote them secretly and convinced Shakespeare to pretend to be the author. They suggest that the Earl of Oxford, Sir Francis Bacon, or even Queen Elizabeth herself wrote Shakespeare's plays.

Historians do not take these theories seriously. Those who knew and worked with Shakespeare during his lifetime never doubted that he had written these plays. No amount of education could have given him his high intelligence, amazing memory, artistic sensitivity, imagination, and profound understanding of the human heart. Just to know him was to realize the genius he was. "He was not for an age," wrote his friend Ben Jonson, "but for all time."

Seven years after Shakespeare's death, in 1623, the first book of his collected plays was published. The world has been reading and performing his plays ever since.

Postscript

Every author wants to make sure that all the facts in the book are correct and that all the words are spelled right. But when writing a book about Shakespeare, spelling is not a simple matter. The reason why makes an interesting story in itself.

In the year 1066, the Normans came over from France and conquered England. For over three hundred years, French was the court language, and English was spoken only by peasants. It wasn't until 1415 that the kings of England began speaking English again, and by then the language had greatly changed. The French spoken by the nobility had come to be more like English, and the English of the common people was full of French words.

People in those days rarely traveled. They spent their whole lives in the same village where their parents and grandparents had lived. And so each region developed its own way of speaking English. William Caxton wrote in 1490 about some sailors from London who were sailing down the Thames River. Fifty miles from London, they came ashore to buy food. They particularly wanted some eggs, which they called "eggys." The farmer's wife, who couldn't understand what they were asking for, assumed they were speaking French. In her village, eggs were "eyren."

Most people couldn't read or write, and those who could simply spelled words the way they pronounced them. If people who lived only fifty miles apart had trouble understanding one another, imagine how many different ways there were of saying—and spelling—even the most common words! There was no regular system of spelling or punctuation, and neither the people of England nor the printers of books seemed to think it was important how words were spelled. On the title page of the first English dictionary, *A Table Alphabeticall of Hard Words* by Robert Cawdrey, published in 1604, the word *words* was spelled two different ways. It was another fifty years before some kind of standard English spelling was established.

People were not even consistent in the way they spelled their own or other people's names. Was Will Kempe's name spelled "Kempe" or "Kemp"? The answer is both. Shakespeare's name has been spelled more than eighty different ways, including "Shagspeare," "Shakspere," and even "Shakestaffe." There are six documents signed by Shakespeare, and he spells his name differently in each one. In his will, he spells it two different ways—"Shakspere" in one place and "Shakspeare" in another. He never signed it "Shakespeare," but over the years, that spelling has been agreed upon, and so it is spelled today.

As there weren't dictionaries and grammar books to keep the language in any particular form, it grew and changed rapidly. People were constantly making up new words—between ten and twelve thousand of them in the years between 1500 and 1650. Shakespeare was a great inventor of words. *Majestic, countless, hint, hurry, reliance, leapfrog, lonely, gust, excellent,* and *gloomy* are only a few of the nearly two thousand words he created.

Shakespeare also found new and vivid ways of describing things. Many of his phrases are so commonly used today that people have no idea they came from his pen. If you have said you were "tongue-tied" or lived in a "fool's paradise"; if you refused to "budge an inch," said that you had "seen better days," or insisted on "fair play"; if you "played fast and loose" or were stung with "green-eyed jealousy"; if you "danced attendance" on your "lord and master" or "suspected foul play" because someone was "as dead as a doornail"; if even your "own flesh and blood" "set your teeth on edge," and you planned to "lie low" until "the crack of doom"; if "the game is up" and, "without rhyme or reason" and "at one fell swoop," you decide to "give the devil his due"; if you call someone an "eyesore" or a "laughing stock," and you decide to "bid him good riddance" and "send him packing"; if you say you have "slept not one wink," "led a charmed life," or "laughed yourself into stitches"; if you feel that it's "high time" that "the truth were known," and it's a "foregone conclusion" that something has "melted into thin air"; then "the long and the short of it" is, "as good luck would have it" and "the truth will out"—you have quoted Shakespeare!

Bibliography

*Brown, John Russell: *Shakespeare and His Theatre*. New York: Lothrop, Lee & Shepard Books, 1982.

Bryson, Bill: *The Mother Tongue: English and How It Got That Way*. New York: William Morrow, 1990.

Fido, Martin: *Shakespeare*. New York: Peter Bedrick Books, 1985.

Folger Shakespeare Library, Volunteer Docents: *Shakespeare for the Young Reader: A Guide to Available Sources*. Washington: 1985.

Fraser, Russell: *Young Shakespeare*. New York: Columbia University Press, 1988.

*Garfield, Leon: *Shakespeare Stories*. New York: Schocken Books, 1985.

Greer, Germaine: *Shakespeare*. Oxford and New York: Oxford University Press, 1986.

*Haines, Charles: *William Shakespeare and His Plays*. New York: Franklin Watts, Inc., 1968.

*Hodges, C. Walter: *Shakespeare's Theatre*. New York: Coward, McCann & Geoghegan, Inc., 1964.

McCrum, Robert, William Cran, and Robert MacNeil: *The Story of English*. New York: Viking, 1986.

Rowse, A. L.: *Shakespeare the Man*. New York: Harper & Row, 1973.

Schoenbaum, S.: *William Shakespeare: A Compact Documentary Life*. New York: Oxford University Press, 1977.

————: *Shakespeare: The Globe and the World*. New York: Folger Shakespeare Library and Oxford University Press, 1979.

*Stewart, Philippa: *Shakespeare and His Theatre*. London: Wayland Publishers, 1973.

*These books will be helpful to young readers interested in further research.

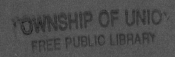